Journey of the Hats

Simple Wisdom from a Grateful Heart

Petronilla Stainbrook

Copyright © 2013 by Petronilla Stainbrook

All rights reserved. No part of this publication may be reproduced, distributed, or transmitted in any form or by any means, including photocopying, recording, or other electronic or mechanical methods, without the prior written permission of the publisher

ISBN-10: 1478233850
ISBN-13: 978-1-47823-385-5

Stainbrook, Petronilla, 1927-
1.Psychology. 2.Poetry. 3.Faith.

Contributions:

Editor: Barbara J. Morse

Title: Jacki O'Donnell

Photography:
Interior: Theresa Mata.
Children: Davin Lucas, Ariah Mata ,Sofia Mata

Cover: Joel Stainbrook,
Dominique Lucas (*Fall Child Photography)*

Printed by Amazon
Made in U.S.A. Charleston, S.C.

Dedication

TO the many special people who have lived this book with me over the years - my thanks. Without your faith and support these pages would still be a pile of notes and poems tucked away with only dream value.   Dear family, friends, mentors, and clients, you have enriched my life, my spirit.

I Dedicate this Book to You!!

A special thanks to each of you, my readers of Journey of the Hats. Hopefully, a thought or two will enrich your lives and help you discover a new or deeper sense of who you are, whatever hat you may be wearing. Joy to you!

Petronilla (Pat)

CONTENTS

MY HATS

My classy mother taught me the joy of hats
They have become a part of who I am
They make me smile

I wear them out to lunch
To church and to the market
I wear them out walking in the rain

People tell me that I have a face
That compliments a hat
I know that I have a spirit that adds
      to their charm

My closet holds all shapes and colors
Some were found in nearby discount stores
Others in fancy shops or distant lands

Men often compliment my hats
Women often wonder why I wear them
It matters not

I feel truly real, truly me
They are my friends
Every day they make me smile

My Hats!

DEAR READER

THIS book speaks of a journey that each
of us is taking. It is called *Life*. The hats that
we wear on this adventure are many. Think
of yourself and the multiple hats you wear as
a son or daughter, husband or wife, brother
or sister, student or teacher, parent or child,
leader or follower, doctor or patient. How
many hats do you wear at the same time?
How many times do you change hats along
with your thoughts, feelings, and actions?

Each of our journeys are unique and cannot
be measured. We cannot measure pain or
perfection nor can we define success or
failure. Only our inner spirit can gauge
peace or sorrow. Our journey is ours alone.

These pages describe elements of some chapter of our lives. Though our realities are solely our own, many of our struggles hold the same fears, the same unknowns, and the same pain. Our challenge is to believe that we always have a choice of how we find meaning in this journey we call life.

I share here my personal poetry - written in joyful times, in lonely and frightened times - as well as a lifetime of professional thoughts that they may add energy to your path.

Using simple words, I present these pages by choosing topics that I believe are critical for study, meditation, and action. Each chapter begins with the definition of key words in the hope that they may add clarity and meaning to the thoughts that follow.

We explore ourselves - one step at a time

1

DISCOVERING SELF

OUR journey of the hats begins with our earliest memories. Everything we touch becomes a discovery of self. As we grow, our life journey becomes more complicated. It leads us in many directions as we explore our emotions, intellect, sexuality, spirituality, and our physical self.

Discovery: awaken to, explore
Message: acquired information, advice
Whole Self: entire natural, essential human qualities

Those who teach us influence our thinking and our actions. Some of the early messages and behaviors that we observe are unhealthy. Some we do not understand or misinterpret. Words like *you're wrong, be careful, you should* confuse our reality. In time, we begin to determine that our self discovery depends on choosing our own beliefs carefully with head and heart.

We begin to learn that we have the power to keep the positive lessons and discard those that come from misguided beliefs. We also learn that many of the messages given by the world around us are not based on knowing us and often not caring for us.

As our world grows wider, our best efforts are sometimes met with failure and disappointment in ourselves.

We learn, however, that mistakes often make us wiser and stronger. We learn what responsibility means and how important it is in our lives. We begin to understand that honesty, hard work, and hope can open new doors for us. Study, prayer, meditation, and outside support are tools available to us. Discovering our talents leads to greater self worth. Courage, creativity and discovery of our self strengthens us on many levels.

This journey also teaches us that life delivers paths that we cannot control. As we mature, we struggle to find direction, peace, and happiness. We often realize the messages that our family, our world, our experiences gave can still control us. These messages (positive and negative) can come alive without our conscious awareness.

By understanding the source and reason behind the endless messages, we learn that we can choose to embrace or reject them. The importance of keeping an eye on our thoughts, our balance, and our interaction with others is paramount. Although it is easy to get caught up in old dreams, the world changes. We change. Yesterday is gone, tomorrow is not a reality. Today can be our focus. How we develop more understanding of self and of others is a daily part of our lifelong journey.

Why do we often resist self examination or change? An honest look at our biases, our resistance to learning, and our refusal to grow is often governed by fear. Are we afraid of the emotions that may arise?

Perhaps we are not aware that our unfinished pain may be hurting others whom we wish to understand and love.

In seeking those who think in different ways from ours, we can often learn from each other. It is never too late to take a new path to self discovery. It is never too late to give up old messages and create new ones. Each of us changes as does the world around us. We can put fear aside, our hiding places aside (e.g., silence, work, perfection, control) to reexamine who we are, where we are.

Discovery and development of our total self - emotional, intellectual, spiritual , sexual, and physical - is our life's adventure. We can use our unique energy from youth to guide us through our aging years. To quote a dear friend, "We can have a zest for life!"

LET'S GO FOR IT

Let's go for life together, my daughters

Let's go for our greatest potential to be
　　truly human

Let's go for our total womanhood in
　　body, mind, spirit, emotion

Let's go for loving ourselves, loving
　　others, loving our life

Let's go for keeping reality alive
　　With sails of dreams
　　With dreams anchored to a harbor of
　　reality

Let's go for it, my beautiful daughters

Let's go for life!

PAINT YOUR WORLD

Every day an adventure in living
Paint your world with you!

Paint your world with caring and
　　forgiving
Paint your world with optimism and
　　creativity
Paint your world with wisdom, courage
　　and joy

When your world disapproves of you
　　causing fear and sadness and confusion
Let it not keep you down
Cry, scream, write, or pray

Paint your world with choosing what is best
Paint your world with the experience of a
　　good life
Paint your world feeling the love of a friend
And, always with gratitude for life

Make every day the best one yet.
Paint your world with you!

*The complexity of nature mirrors
our journey*

2

UNDERSTANDING THE TASK

AS we pursue our discovery of self, we ask ourselves what knowledge we have to guide us. Studying our "total self" begins to teach us of both our strengths as well as the lesser developed parts of ourselves. *Intellectually,* we can pursue constant learning. We have many tools to do so - being aware, reading, schooling, feedback from wise persons, our own experiences, etc. No matter how we choose to capture or share it with others, learning is the core of life.

Intellectual: reasonable, perceptive, educated
Physical: body strength, health
Emotional: natural range of feelings
Sexual/Sensual: physical perception; e.g., sight, touch, taste
Spiritual: inner faith, beyond conscious

Recognizing and accepting our weakest areas can be fearful, yet the results can be incredibly freeing. We have only one life, and only one chance to live it fully.

Our *Physical Self* asks that we care for our bodies. Much is written concerning weight, exercise, rest, vitamins, etc. We learn to determine what is best for ourselves while having consideration for others. There is no single method that fits us all. Balancing whatever we do physically is an important key to health. Extremes rarely succeed. We can be influenced physically in a positive or negative way by our emotional messages and expression. Our minds and our bodies are closely and clearly connected and this is quite often demonstrated in our health.

Our *Emotional* self is complex involving a wide range of feelings. It is the expression of these feelings that creates positive or negative consequences. Extremes of any emotion can cause pain to ourselves and others.

Two of the most powerful emotions are fear and anger. Healthy fear protects us from harm. It can, however, prevent our creativity, our sense of adventure, our learning. Anger , in turn, often covers loss and sadness and can prevent understanding, forgiveness, and peace. If we search for and find the roots of fear and anger, we will loosen their mental and physical control. Confidence and well-being can be gained.

Hiding emotions with fear or anger makes our journey of life more complicated. Our culture's understanding of emotion has much to learn - judgment of what is acceptable or healthy permeates our Western beliefs. As such, we must chart our own course in developing emotional maturity and peace.

Our *Sensual/Sexual* self includes each of our senses: smell, taste, hearing, touch, sight. Awareness and use of each sense meets our need for safety and freedom. They also meet our need for warmth and beauty. In sharing our sexuality with another person, each of our senses becomes part of that human choice. Extremes regarding our sensual/sexual expression may result in physical, emotional, and spiritual pain.

Our *Spiritual* self is a longer, deeper discovery. It is developed through life experiences, deep awareness, meditation and/or prayer. The teachings received by participation in a particular faith can set a stage for our discovery of spiritual self. We must, however, develop this gift in our own way and at our own time in our journey. Looking beyond our humanness to a deeper consciousness enriches our entire self.

In addition to our intellectual, physical, emotional, sensual/sexual, and spiritual selves, we need *connection* on many levels - personally, socially, and professionally. It is difficult to face the fear of rejection, judgment, or failure that may result as we attempt to connect. At these times it is easy to retreat, make excuses or give up.

One of the primary ways to connect is through communication. This is an art that we can develop as we search for our needs in any situation. When communicating it is essential to try to understand the person with whom we are attempting to make the connection. Words are powerful and quite often misunderstood.

In addition, there are many people in our world who do not know how or do not wish to connect with one another. As difficult as it is, we need to control our own emotions in this regard. Accepting this situation helps us set a limit in our effort to communicate and connect and/or move on in another direction.

Maintaining an ongoing connection with family is a stronghold in life. As part of a family, one sets the stage for learning to love self and life. A family is a mirror for each of us. Even when the mirror is cracked, we can sometimes step through that disadvantage to understanding and forgiveness.

The journey of understanding ourselves and others can be intriguing. It can fill our lives with riches. We can choose to blame our parents, our genes, our country, or anyone and anything that gives us reason to stop our path towards understanding ourselves and living a fulfilling life. Doing so, we often escape life – choosing ignorance, doubt, and pain. We often hide behind the unknown and attempt to control the present.

Choosing these paths for our lives will not lead us to the happiness and peace that we all deserve. However, when we do the hard work to understand who we are and what we believe our life is about, we feel confidence and self worth. Only then are we open to a full life of giving to ourselves and others!

FREEDOM

To be free is not what it seems.
It appears to be having our own way,
    our own desires.
It appears to be wiser and stronger than
    another.
It appears to be unattached to limits,
    commitment or responsibility to
    others.

Freedom is not these things.
But rather it is:
    A powerful feeling and belief in
    ourselves,
    Where we are going and why we are
    here.

It is choosing to share our journey with
others --
    Caring, not injuring
    Staying, not retreating
    Forgiving, not judging

Freedom is choosing to love.

THIS I BELIEVE

I believe in the miracle of wisdom and
    learning

I believe in celebrating every moment of life

I believe in the miracle of life with its tiny
    joys

I believe in the unexplainable greatness of
    persons

I believe in never giving up, helping each other
to find strength

    Strength to grow
    Strength to bear the pain and loss
    Strength to go beyond the fear

I believe that our births were meant to
    change the human condition, bit by bit,
    with goodness

I believe that we are meant to give hope
    and to teach love

I believe that our lives will ebb and flow
    with pain and joy with those we love
    and the lives we touch

A BOX

Don't put me in a box by judging me
You know so little of who I am
Of what I believe, of what I feel
Of where I am or where I choose to go

You know so little of my faith or how I
    pray
Accept my strengths without competition
Accept my weaknesses , knowing your
    own
Accept my smile, my touch ,as a gift

Don't put me in a box

Learn with me
Give to me and receive from me
Connect with me

Don't put me in a box

Like our mountains, our life's path is often steep and challenging

3

DEVELOPING A MISSION

CHOOSING how we wish to live our lives is an ongoing challenge. Awareness of our talents and our blessings allows us to use them both realistically and creatively. Defining our goals in spite of the odds (e.g., lack of knowledge, health, or circumstances) is within our power. If our direction is guided by learning, self-confidence, love, and faith, these cornerstones can conquer many difficult outside influences. Our inner fears and doubts will no longer control us.

Mission: design, direction, purpose
Challenge: confront, question, risk
Choice: select, decide, free will
Loneliness: lacking human energy or direction

We often believe that we have no choice or free will and that outside factors control our lives. However, we can gain the mental, emotional, and spiritual strength to develop positive action. Creative thinking and outside support are particularly critical at this juncture.

Often our early mission is chosen by our immaturity or by the needs of others. As we gain self-worth, we may realize that our present course is not fulfilling. Establishing a new mission is possible at any age if done wisely. It is a step in leading a meaningful life. However, change is extremely difficult and complicated. It can be uncomfortable and fearful especially in the early stages. Many of us have been taught that it is not wise to risk new thinking or new action.

This period of flux becomes a time of guidance, quiet personal appraisal, and prayer. Feedback from experienced persons is critical. Naturally, no one person, wise professional, trusted friend, or family member can decide our choices for us. They can, however, share and encourage. They can add balance to our thinking and be our cheerleaders in the process.

Even when in a positive place, choices are sometimes limited. We need to evaluate all the factors that may influence our movement in a different direction. For example, what impact will our decision have on others in our life? What positives are we losing or successes are we gaining? We often have little to lose and much to gain by risking a new direction in our lives.

Our mission is sometimes shortsighted. It may be developed seeking financial wealth, power, or personal recognition - not acknowledging our need for emotional and spiritual development or the high price we may eventually pay. We become the roles we play. Finding our own peaceful self or improving our world are often seldom considered. Of course, we all seek freedom, safety, and enjoyment in our lives. It is the excess of any part of our mission that creates imbalance and pain. A wise young man shared these words with me. "I was chasing financial success and found it, but I learned it gave little to my spirit." With a great deal of effort, he dramatically changed his mission and became a teacher to others.

Let us keep our direction clear. Our mission is one that *we* choose. Working from our head while neglecting our hearts can be a derailing factor in our journey. The opposite can also be true - leading from our heart without a balance of wisdom and reality can impede our journey. Only we have the wisdom or responsibility for our day to day choices. We must try to carefully, wisely, and creatively chart our course.

A Zest for Life

They say she has a zest for life
She contemplates the meaning
Is it her smile, her energy
Her positive approach to her world?

Little do they know of her pain
Of early loss, of later sadness
She learned to smile, to hide it well
By giving and touching others

Slowly she learned to care for self
And find a balanced way to live -
One of interaction with those
Whose lives she touched

Celebrating her zest for life!

Amtrak Melody

The humming tracks sing the melody
River bubbling through frozen waters
Spring struggling for birth
Softly whispering new life

Animals now unseen, hidden and warm
Pines still burdened with snow
Groves of aspen, sleeping until summer

And soon ,shades of green
Tiny creatures reclaiming their homes
Grazing livestock running free
The eagle arrives to greet them all

Old villages alive to the simple living
Treasuring their nest, the quiet beauty
To plant again and harvest the earth
These mountain people smile

Smile at the indescribable peaks
Their rocks as if painted there
Awesome, sculptured passes
Early travelers challenged by each

Smile knowingly at billowing clouds
Reaching upward to unknown places
Low grasses and deep gorges
Beauty of the morning, the sunsets

I fantasize the early traveler
Seeker of freedom, of wealth
The whistle awakens me to
Deep emotions, to grateful peace

'Tis an Amtrak melody

*As our life flows on, we test
deeper emotions*

4

RISKING A CONNECTION

WE humans have always sought connection. When we are young, gaining this natural need is safe and easy. However, slowly but surely, the larger world brings fear into our lives. As we experience rejection and misunderstanding, we lose the confidence of being vulnerable.

Connecting means knowing and understanding the other, which is often very difficult. We try to do so long before we understand ourselves, our emotions, our strengths , or our undeveloped selves.

Connection: interdependent, unite, link
Vulnerable: showing deep self, exposed
Creative: original, imaginative
Understanding: find out, grasp

Connecting means being vulnerable even when our emotions are most fragile. Connecting means communication where words are so often misunderstood. Occasionally, we are fortunate to have persons in our lives that know how to reach out to us without judgment. Through them we learn how to trust and communicate. Through trial and error we learn how important it is to master this element of life with others.

A multiple of human needs are satisfied with and by others. Our parents, teachers, our employers, a variety and skilled and caring persons are essential in our life's journey. Building a network with neighbors, friends, and a host of persons whose lives we touch becomes a treasure to all of us.

Developing friendships, in particular, have a great deal to teach us. In seeking connection, we learn from others and can become more secure. These friendships may afford us a new way of experiencing life, of learning more about ourselves. Wise friendships empower us, add to our strengths, challenge us, teach us. They are invaluable. A deep friendship has the power of meeting our need for connection.

We are often limited , however, by our lack of life experience - our reality is often misguided and we make poor choices in connecting with others. Sadly, we all have experienced times when we have been let down by one another. Mixed messages and unrealistic expectations disconnect us causing anger, sadness, and disappointment.

We must learn to forgive ourselves and others, which is extremely difficult because the world does not teach us this great strength. Blaming others, our parents, our genes, or our circumstances for our failed connections is of no value to us. Unless we attempt to understand and forgive, we are paralyzed to move forward. Anger, blame, and hopelessness take away our power to be creative and to make new choices.

How can we proceed during these difficult times? Avoiding extremes, reaching out to trusting and encouraging people rebuilds our self worth and releases our creative spirit. While "connecting" via technological devices may save us time, these tools cannot replace the human voice or touch.

They cannot personally connect us with those who may greatly influence our emotional or spiritual self. Connection is the core of life!

The Connection of Tears

Today our connection is broken
The coming together that often comes
    easily is so difficult today

Help me understand your struggle
    The fear and sadness
    that is also mine

The world has drawn us apart
Now seeing this, we listen
    we understand,
    we begin again

Suddenly it happens --
    we let each other in
Our wisdom and our tears
Have made a connection of love

Christmas Night

They came bearing gifts
Chosen from their hearts
For their Father and I
And for one another

How different they are
These grown children of ours
Coming from the same home
Where they were all loved

How alike they are
Though raised in different times
Absorbing different lessons
From the 50's to the 70's

Tonight they come
Caring and loving each other
So different they are but so alike
So loved this Christmas night!

Family

Born to be loved, their first born son
These idealizing parents, blessed with hope
Clinging together in their innocence
       A Family

Three daughters filled their dreams
Filled their lives loving them all
Challenging them all
        Their Family

Too soon the world brought pressures
Brought doubt, loneliness, and pain
To each in different ways
       This Family

Yet they struggled through and learned
Forgave and chose to love
With paths of awareness and celebration
       A Growing Family

They had each other
Clinging together in the wounded times
Not always agreeing, but accepting
Not always sure, but hopeful
Believing, cheering, grateful
       This Caring Family

Challenging one another with what they knew
Knowing that they knew so little
Faith hey had and perseverance
       A Trusting Family

Family, cont.

And, now each of them is grown
Knowing success and loss, knowing life
Carving their lives and new families
            Growing Family

Finding friendships and understanding
What it takes to love self and others
Knowing that dreams and words are easy
But that loving is hard
            Our Family

Home

Home is where you can be silent...
        And still be heard
Where you can ask and find out
Who you are and where you're headed

Home is where people laugh with you,
        About you
Home is where sorrow is divided and joy
        Multiplied
Home is a long bath and fresh sheets

Home is an aroma of hot chocolate
        And peanut butter cookies
Home is where there aren't enough bathrooms
        And too many people talking at once
Home is where you learn about living and dying

Peaceful moments help us gain balance

5

EMBRACING THE JOURNEY

OUR journey can be seen as fate. It can also be seen as a gift. How we embrace life depends on many factors - especially how we decide to develop ourselves, how to learn from others, and how to avoid the negative messages that we receive. Messages such as, *you can't, you have to, you're not smart enough*, (or talented enough, too young, to old, and on and on). Why should we listen? Why should we allow these cultural messages to control us? If we have a plan for our journey, we can make it our own.

Embrace: welcome, adapt, enfold
Journey: quest, adventure
Change: adjust, replace, alter
Culture: cumulated beliefs by society, world at large

Embracing the journey asks of us a life of learning. We are taught in so many ways, by so many people and so many circumstances. Friends, old and new, or those unlike ourselves, teach us a great deal. They are like mirrors for us to examine ourselves without fear. They accept us for who we are, understand our struggles, and give us honest feedback. They celebrate our successes. These persons may be our parents, teachers, or siblings. They may even be strangers, if we are open to their messages.

Travel , near or far , can open our eyes to a world unlike our own. Through our travels, we can be challenged to learn and to enrich our thinking and creativity.

Looking at ourselves on a regular basis as we relate to others socially, emotionally, and spiritually continues to be a necessary ingredient of our journey. The world changes, we change, circumstances change - all alter our road map of life. If, however, we accept the changes , we can learn new coping skills and make choices that enable us to move forward and embrace life.

Encountering people who have embraced a most difficult journey with grace and creativity teach us from their example. Too often, we become fearful and selfish. We take on the *Why me?* thinking. A dear, young friend who fought cancer for several years before dying displayed throughout her illness both courage and acceptance. She often remarked, "Why *not* me?"

 It can be difficult to carve out the time to encounter our own feelings or thoughts. Many times it seems easier to ignore, deny, or settle for the sadness and pain. We must look to our own wisdom in assessing our journey and making the new choices needed. If driving, we came upon a broken bridge, we would change our direction. Should we not examine our life's route in the same way?

Each day, sometimes many times a day, we need to practice forgiveness. We have not been given many tools or models to learn how to forgive. As we are judged unfairly, rejected, ignored, or emotionally injured, anger and sadness arises. There are many ways to deal with this pain – pain arising from relationships of all kinds and pain from simply living life.

Carrying resentment and emotional hurt from these encounters can be debilitating - taking action is very important. Physical activity, journaling, prayer, or sharing the pain with someone you trust will be the foundation for understanding the situation. Only then can you forgive and be at peace.

If something is so ugly, so inhumane, that we cannot understand or forgive, it need not ruin our lives. We can choose to distance ourselves from the pain by doing for others.

We each struggle with life in many ways - from youth to old age. By deciding to learn together, to embrace our strengths and help one another, to share and compromise, our world can be a peaceful one. We can embrace our journey with gratitude and love.

Travel Unraveled

Confusion, long lines, frantic voices
Cramped seats, hurried hostesses,
Numbed passengers, weary faces
Missed flights, long ramps, lost luggage
Costly food, rushing crowds

So little grace, so little warmth
The excitement of travel gone
The ease of travel gone

The person a number, a plastic card
A way of life today
True joy of travel gone

Yet, we chose the challenge
To know the world beyond us
To know its past, to relish its beauty
To learn its struggles, its creative power

It can teach us, inspire us
We must accept the physical price we pay
We must focus on the adventure we seek
In this world, so changed,
    our spirits survive

Awesome City

Between the mountains
Clouds hide you as we approach
In the sky above you
    Awesome Mexico City

Un-countable homes and taxis
Wonderful markets and parks
Contain your people

Huge city pulsing below us
Unreal the energy it holds
Wealth, poverty, sadness, joy

Seemingly double decked
So close the homes, the streets
No spot empty of life

Now green patches appear
Children playing, lovers touching
A multitude of souls and spirits

Endless miles your city stretches
Endless years your city records
We come to know your yesterday
    And your today

Show us your treasures
Teach us your history
Except us as friends
    Awesome Mexico City

Beautiful Spanish Face

Beautiful Spanish face, with lovely eyes
Eyes that speak of mystery

Reserved Spanish face, thoughtful
Pensive voice reaching out in English

Classic Spanish face, chiseled features
Chiseled with graceful style

Romantic Spanish face, carefully carved
Hiding the warmth within

Lovely Spanish face, sheltering
Gentleness inside, shyness inside

Beautiful Spanish woman, speak to me
Smile and trust my warm American spirit
Help me know your country
Born before Christ
Guide me through my wonderment
Of your entrancing world

Captured by your beautiful, Spanish Face!

Oh, Manhattan

Oh, Manhattan, city of endless lights
Seen by two wide-eyed women,
In awe of the intense energy
Where all your senses come alive

In awe of the naked sadness
And the breathtaking wonders
As the endless lights appear
As the subway rushes underground

The parks and shops, the food, the taxis
Towering buildings, stacked together
The people's spirits touch you
As they rush by the amazed women

Moving closer, braving the unknown
Surrounded by this mass of humanity
Frightened by this place
Yet stirred by their adventures

The city shocks, scatters your mind
Takes away your breath
Overwhelms you, embraces you
Challenges you to go on

Rallying forth, these women find
New adventure at every turn
Sights and sounds never known
Portrait of the whole of humanity

This magic city that never sleeps
Opens new wonders of life
Opens awareness of your need
Need for learning and friendship
Need for challenge, adventure, magic

Oh, Manhattan

Our lives draw meaning from the
awesome beauty of the changing leaves

6

CREATING A BALANCE

DIFFICULT as it is to find a balance in this fast moving world, we must search for it. It is a great gift to give to ourselves. We need to take the time to slow down, to tune out the noise and listen to our inner spirit. We don't need a cave or a monastery to find our own balance. We simply need to see its importance, choose it, and find realistic ways to claim it.

Control: power, force, repress
Balance: equalize, to use head and heart
Extreme: excessive, unreasonable
Awareness: insight, open to, perceptive

Balance shows itself in peaceful responses amid mass confusion. It shows itself when our strength overcomes pain and loss. It shows itself when we dismiss doubt, fear, and judgment. It becomes our guide in making the best choices even when all the odds are against us.

And, there *are* many odds against us in our journey to find balance , especially shown in the messages of "extremes". Every form of government and religion, every type of education and business - even our personal health and family lives - have been affected by extreme beliefs. We are told that we are not pretty enough, intelligent enough, healthy enough, wealthy enough, or spiritual enough. We know that there is no right answer that fits every individual.

However, the multiple messages we receive often change overnight and are so powerful that one finds balanced thinking or balanced choice very difficult. If we honestly look at our own small world, we discover choices that we have made that were out of balance - choices which brought sadness to ourselves and those close to us.

What role do we play in finding a peaceful balance? As our lives change in a dramatically changing world, we have great reason to try to keep our balance. We have been blessed with remarkable technical advances that have no doubt only begun. It is easy to see that our personal lives have been affected. Let us ask ourselves if using these devices and/or media aimed at instant communication add balance to our lives.

Have we permitted this technology to replace more intimate ways of communicating? What wonderful, old values have we lost in our rush for the new? Are we aware that our amazing technical advances can overcome our common sense? The messages we receive are too often misunderstood or poorly communicated.   Unless we are aware of what we may be losing (not just gaining) with any new discovery, we lose our balance.

 Being aware of both the positive and negative implications of our choices is critically important. We are a people of study, judgment, and reflection. Our strength and inner peace has always been gained by balancing mind and heart.

Guardians of 17th

Below a clear, magenta sky they tower
   and wave
These stately spruce, all old and majestic
Holding family secrets in their branches
The guardians of 17th

Above the tender grasses
   The hot pavement
   The screeching sirens
   The sleeping babe
These beauties keep watch

Fanning our pain, caressing our nest,
   celebrating our joys
These majestic branches stand
In beauty of the avenue
In symbol of our dreams

The guardians of 17th

Rocky Mountain Beauty

The giants wake gently
    In the mist of morning Beauty
Their shadows become real
    And take their bow
White beast and bird soar to greet them
The rising sun signals them
    And they respond
Becoming clearer by the moment
Massive stretch of rock and snow
    Choose the day
The forest kneels beneath them
    Sheltering the tiny ones
On frozen ground this March morn
    Rocky Mountain beauty
The quiet enfolds my spirit
    And frees my mind
The look is pure
Encircling me with peace
The glory of the sun's touch
Peaks over the western range
    Lighting the sky
    Warming the mountain
Deeply it embraces the slopes
And dances toward the east
    What a gift you are
Dear Rocky Mountain beauty

Our Quickie Guests

It always happens when I've just begun
To clean cupboards or defrost the 'frig
When my hair is limp and my energy low

The call from the airport - friends in town
Would we have time with them
We need to be humble, or is it hysterical

We tell these old friends we'd be delighted to
Pick them up, have dinner and spend the night
An hour (drive slowly dear) to clear the decks

I know I need a small army to assist me
I am an army of One
The 'frig is reassembled, frost and all

I change the sheets and comb my hair
My hysteria is calmed by my creativity
Our car announces their arrival

Their bedroom welcomes
Dinner is in motion
My smile hides the whirlwind hour

We welcome these old friends
Our quickie guests

*During our journey of life, we seek
harmony and peace*

7

KNOWING ACCEPTANCE

FEW of us have been taught how to except what we cannot change. We have not learned that change and loss are a constant part of life. Though we may experience loss in our youth (e.g., a first love, a team position, a job), the fortunate ones among us are protected by family or kind friends. Later in life, our losses become much deeper - some life changing. As these changes occur, we often have little knowledge, support, or experience of how to recover from them.

Forgiveness: let go, free, open-hearted
Loss: sacrifice, grief, death
Acceptance: believe, adapt, affirm
Meditation/prayer: reflect, silent looking inward

How can we teach ourselves that acceptance and forgiveness are critical to peaceful living and loving? Can we accept that happiness is fashioned from an inside awareness and choice, not from outside messages? Our inner fears - loss of youth, fear of rejection, of being alone or unloved - need not control us. Society escalates these fears in so many ways. While it is hard to escape the messages of how we should look, think, love, or pray we need to discover what drummer we march to. What set of messages do we live by? What attitudes do we have - what fears, what expectations? Does our daily life allow balanced decisions or does it close off our confidence and hope? If we choose to learn the art of acceptance, we open the door to new ways of thinking, learning, and healing, allowing us to fully embrace life.

The art of acceptance is extremely complicated. It takes a great deal of thought, study, creativity, and introspection to learn how to accept. What is healthy acceptance? It is wisely using the tools of compromise, and balance to change what is possible. Each of us have more positive power than we realize. We cannot change the many cultural messages, but we can accept them for what they are. We cannot control tomorrow but we can make a positive impact on today.

By sharing our fears and our pain with a trusting person, we balance our thinking and stand a good chance of choosing healthy acceptance. Acting alone rarely results in a healthy outcome. Alone it is easier to escalate our pain, blame others ,and spend our lives escaping in one way or another.

It is difficult to *accept love* today. So many people have been emotionally injured while trying to love or be loved by another. They face the fears of attempting to build a life with anyone. It is wise to direct our energy to our own development at this time. Have we understood and finished our old wounds ? Do we have unrealistic expectations of others? Have we evaluated our manner of communication and control? Can we forgive, compromise, and support the needs of another? Can we separate minor differences from life changing ones? Let us look at our complete self:

Intellectual: have we developed our minds and our awareness of total self?

Emotional: have we learned to understand our emotional self and how to share feelings with another?

Physical: have we taken care of our bodies and know how to use them wisely?

Spiritual: have we learned of our inner goodness? Meditation and prayer can help us keep in touch with our spirit and the power beyond our human consciousness.

Learning about and more fully knowing our complete self gives us the tools to choose wisely, overcome fear, trust in spite of the unknowns , and accept love.

One of our most difficult challenges is the ability to *accept loss*. Actually, we lose every day, perhaps many times a day. We lose our success in things large and small; we make mistakes. We lose our youth, strength, insight, understanding, and positive control in one way or another. Loss is part of life.

As healthy creatures we concentrate on life. We give little thought to death. We are often not prepared for this dramatic ending of life. It challenges us beyond description even if we know it is inevitable. Surely, our "stay young forever" culture does little to prepare us. Realistically, the years do not stand still. Life changes. We change. Life is lost in one way or another - our physical strength, our mental keenness, our friends, our support systems are all affected by loss. As we age and experience loss, our whole social network can feel strange and uncomfortable, and sometimes fearful.

Our culture often gives a message of getting through loss as quickly as possible. Many believe drugs will resolve the pain of loss and spare them from feeling the loss so deeply.

Although sometimes needed short term, drugs only to serve to cover the deeper pain or send it underground. It does not matter if we think of death in abstract or spiritual terms, our human spirit is deeply affected when death becomes a reality.

If we accept life along the way, we are more likely to see death as the end of our human chapter. While we can ignore it, struggle against it or work through its painful loss, finally, with acknowledgment, we can begin a new chapter with understanding, grace, and acceptance. Let us challenge ourselves to deal with loss in a mature way. It will truly make our lives much richer and more peaceful.

Classy Lady

I miss you, dear classy lady
The morning call, the drop-in times
The connect in prayer
The macaroni, the cookies, and tea

I miss your simple beauty
Your acceptance of life's pain
Your celebration of life's joy

You always made me feel loved
You were and are my cheerleader

You loved the first man in my life
And, later, the man I now love

I miss your hats and your creativity
I miss your naiveté
I miss the realness of you

I am lonely for you
Some moments of every day
I give thanks for you, my Mom

I love you!

A Gift

I was his teacher and his friend
He was my friend and my teacher

I treasure the laughter that we shared
    The ideas we debated
    The dreams of our world

He was an aware, sensitive man
He had a brilliant mind, a caring
    heart

He loved his family every moment
    He respected me
    He respected the truth

I miss experiencing life with him
His spirit will never leave me

A Mother's Love

My daughter is dying
Her every breath is effort
For this woman of energy
Her dear face, expressionless
After short years of loving life

Too young to die, leaving grieving
Lover and precious sons
Leaving brothers and sisters
    Who love her so
Too soon to leave a mourning mother
Who fought to save her for so long

Dear daughter, how can I say goodbye
Holding you, caressing you, touching
    Your aching body
Treasuring every hour being with you

My heart is an open, bleeding place
    As you cling to life
Dressing you, bathing you, praying
Wanting so for you to live

Dear one, we will live on when you go
It will take many moons, many tears
Lonely days until we smile again
We will continue to live with many
Questions of medicine's powerlessness
    And our helplessness

By the Ocean

Here in this majestic spot beside the ocean
    I call your name
Where the only sound is a tiny bird
That might have been a dinosaur
Struck dumb by the vast waters it surveyed

Here on this rustic patio, hung over the Pacific
    I see you walking
No fishing rod could snare a trout here, though
We could heal my pain and trumpet your freedom
Your pain is no more, dear Dad

You slipped into heaven softly in mother's arms
    I feel you
Little treasure did you leave for us to share
With me you left an empty place forever
A combination of bareness and wholeness

I try to push the fog away, but foolish
    I hear your voice
The quiet gives me pause
The ocean appears deeper before my eyes
And now I awake

In this flowered sheeted brass bed
    I sense you are here
The knock, raspberries and cream
Coffee and scrumptious nut bread
I speak to you, dear Dad

The memories remain forever
Your love remains forever
By this awe-inspiring ocean

    I let you go

*Children teach us uncomplicated,
unconditional love*

8

LEARNING TO LOVE

SO much is written concerning love. Each person's idea of love and their expression of love is as diverse as the stars. Love has been analyzed and judged, lived and died for without true definition. We often hear, *love others, love your body, love your home, love your family, love your country.* Love is so complex, it touches every part of our life. It is both a private adventure and a public display.

Love: deep connection, esteem and devotion, loyalty
Compromise: negotiate, middle road, give and take
Learning: gaining knowledge
Escapes: methods to avoid/hide/dodge

When we find someone who adds to our lives in special ways, we call it "falling in love". This is the very time to slow down the fall. It is time to explore our individual missions regarding faith, family, life styles, and goals. Are we willing to blend our beliefs, to learn and grow with each other? Are we willing to compromise our differences?

Building a friendship with a special person is invaluable. It becomes the foundation for a long term relationship. While friendships are formed in many ways and for many reasons, they are always formed to make a connection - a need for any human as they journey through life. With a friend we gain a new way of experiencing life, of learning more of self. Wise friendships empower us, add to our strengths, challenge us, teach us.

We can also learn from the hurtful connections and with support, gain healing and renewed strength.

Choosing to love another is one of the most courageous and complicated undertakings in life. No feelings are more intense, more humbling, or more beautiful than loving and being loved. Neither accomplishment, nor power, nor instant gratification can equal its depth. Children understand it clearly and simply. As adults, we often mistake it for emotions that have little to do with true love. Sensual love is powerful but it is only a piece of knowing how to love completely.

Choosing to love for a lifetime is a mature adventure. It is wise to begin the journey with a secure and confident self-identity.

Unfinished pain, self pity, guilt, and fear bring up extreme emotions and behaviors in an intimate relationship. Little energy remains for the creativity of building a life with another. Our birth family often comes on the scene as does every deep relationship that each of us has experienced. As children, we had little power to separate or understand the messages that we were given. As adults, now free to choose our relationships, we may often encounter confusion, rejection, and pain. However, with determination and support, we can learn to understand and forgive some of these early chapters and begin to build our own path, our own way to love.

Loving relationships may encounter roadblocks and endure setbacks.

Expectations change, not always realistically. Communication can break down and , when left unrepaired, can derail our journey. The addictions of seeking perfection, money or power diminish any relationship. Often struggles with alcohol, drugs, violence, poor health or other issues complicate a long term relationship. The untrue though common message - that we all deserve to be happy and get all of our needs met all of the time - echoes loud and clear. Blaming, escaping in fear rather than seeking understanding and forgiveness, only results in pain.

 However, these difficult times can also signal a new and deeper love. We can learn more of who we are and where we are going together. We can find a new way of loving. We can find joy in simple things.

We can learn the art of forgiveness,
gratefulness, and understanding the needs of
one another. It may take a lifetime to learn.

In a loving relationship, every hat we wear
on our journey is challenged by our new
identity – one that includes *you, me,* and *us.*
In choosing a life together, consider the
following thoughts:

Love has at its core, trusting, touching, and telling
It is giving and forgiving every day, ourselves
      and each other
It is a platform for growth of beliefs and behavior

Love is exploring, risking, and always learning
It is looking in and reaching out
It is not expecting everything
But being grateful for so much

Love is a compromising way of life
Often forgetting yourself for the other
Sharing control, saying "I'm sorry"
And beginning again

Love is believing in a greater
Power beyond our limited awareness

Can we experience loving relationships without a special other? It may be a more complicated journey, but many show us it is not only possible but enormously fulfilling. Connecting with nature and beauty, with learning and giving, with family and children, and with special persons who touch our lives is the platform. As with all relationships, through our giving and receiving we find joy as individuals and experience the warmth that comes only from loving and being loved.

Highway Seventy

Miles of highway spent with you
    Adventuring in the Rockies
    Amid its awesome beauty

Planning these hours with you
    Stealing this special time
    From Monday to Friday days

This time to touch
    To savor words
    To celebrate loving

The highway invites us
    To place still unknown
    Experiences unrehearsed

We discover each other
    Amid these awesome peaks
    As awesome as our next kiss

Highway Seventy do you remember
    The kaleidoscope of hours
    Travelling with you, loving him

Six Loves

We have loved each other, the two of us
Of this love, our four, and those they love
Our Six

Six beautiful grandchildren who share
Their hours with us
They call us Pops and Grandma
And have won our hearts
Our Six

We have held their tiny bodies
Been held by their strong arms
They teach us and trust us
Our door is always open to them
Our Six

They bring us their worries and their pride
Dealing with a most difficulty world
They listen to our past, so different
Fascinating to hear,
Impossible to understand
Our Six

We tell each of them to learn and give
We cheer them and comfort them
Our prayers always follow them
We are grateful for the lives we share
With Our six

Proud Old House

Build a hundred years ago
Bought with love three decades ago
Filled with energy, joyful and sad
    It proudly stands today

The winds embracing its frame
The snows enveloping its body
Surrounded by peaks, the mountain goats
Filled with memories of miners and of gold
    It proudly stands today

While poppies and lilacs greet the spring
Peeling paint begs for renewal
The town frozen in yesterday
With streets unpaved and newness shunned
    The old house proudly stands

So many memories are here, chapters of our
    lives
A lost puppy, you and I alone and close
Long walks to town, riding the train
Card games, ball games, celebrations
    The old house stands

Hamburgers on the grill, homemade ice
    cream
Carmel apples and smores

Proud Old House, cont.

Children camping, Pops attending
Family groups, teaching groups
   The old house stands

Quiet moments, loud gatherings
Late night puzzles and debates
Caring, giving, creating, sharing
A ghost who shared this space
   The proud old house stands

Still giving, this old house
Easing the stress life brings on
But never erasing the wonderful moments
Of family and friends, of living and loving
   This proud old house of memories

Treasures

Not mine to fashion into what I dream
Not mine to design for prideful display
Not mine to judge them right or wrong

But mine to listen and to care
Amid their fears and loneliness
Amid their search for self

Mine to share their lives
Their beauty and their love
On loan to me, these treasures

Reflecting the simple beauty of creation
calms our spirit

9

CREATING INNER PEACE

GAINING inner peace is a gradual and persistent search. In our complicated world our lives can overwhelm us. We may make poor choices as we interact with others. Our human weaknesses may cause us to injure ourselves or others. We often do not recognize what we have done or how to undo our actions. To find inner peace, we need to learn who we are and how we choose to live our lives.

Inner peace: deep-seated, calm serenity
Expectations: anticipate, look forward to
Secure: safe, reliable, confident
Consciousness: awareness, tuned in

Sadly, many of us have been given little guidance or assistance in understanding what life is all about. Our families were often lacking in the knowledge that they had the tools to teach us. We have grown up in a world so different from our parents', how could they have understood what we faced? Institutions of government, education, and religion have become so depersonalized and so large that we are constantly confronted with negative and/or mixed messages.

The inner spirit is so often neglected as it seeks inner peace. Every day we are challenged to understand and to forgive injustice. When we realize that we cannot change the unfairness that surrounds us, we must let it go - not doing so will only injure our minds, bodies, and spirits.

How do we know that our inner peace is at risk? We are often unwilling to face the pain of injustice. We may cover that pain with unrealistic expectations and bad choices. We may lose our balance in thinking and acting clearly. Behaviors such as denial, anger, blaming, retreating, lashing out, and even illness are symptoms that our inner peace is at risk. When we put aside our defenses and accusations, however, we open ourselves to understanding and peace.

There are many ways to set a stage for the development of inner peace. Quiet moments of meditation or prayer can lead us to peace. This deeper state of consciousness puts our minds on hold. It allows our feelings and thoughts to clarify. Balance of our overloaded senses can be restored.

Walking, journaling, music, nature, solitude, and rest quiet the world that so often engulfs us. Being with people and places that shout of hope and beauty also set a stage to maintain inner peace. Forgiveness is an everyday challenge in life. Without forgiveness, we can never find serenity.

Should we assist others in finding inner peace? Is caring not a way to help them? We are not responsible to do their work or to change their thinking or behavior for this is impossible. We can, however, set a stage by modeling a hopeful spirit in their search. We can call it loving. Life passes too quickly to deny ourselves and those whose lives we touch the calm that inner peace can give.

Waiting for the Zephyr

Over the Rockies you come and I wait for you,
    my friend
The station announcing later and later your
    arrival time
Patient souls, babes and grandparents, weary
    warriors
All passing the lengthening time
These friendly folk, frowning folk, sleeping folk,
    playing folk

The smell of popcorn and stale coffee
The sound of a hundred tennis shoes milling
    about
The sight of the world in miniature
A world of good people, caring people
A world of simple people, heading where?

Where are they going? Where have they been?
Whom do they love? Who loves them?

Smiles begin! The Zephyr is arriving on track #2
Few people move from their nests on the benches
Hardly believing it

But my heart is happy
My dear friend is here!

A Cookie Marathon of Love

Our cookie world unfolds
    And tells a story of two lives
Decades of a friendship grown deep
    Celebrated as surely as snow falls this day
In our cookie marathon of love

Wiser and softer we both are
    Stronger and more humble
We laugh more, we pain more
    Because we see now
More truth about ourselves
    And others who touch our lives

The babes have been born
    Grown beautiful and handsome
Their fathers we still choose as lovers
    Pals and sometimes opponents

With Diamond Christmas music
    We've shared loss and fear, joy and blessings
Shared talents and our dreams
    Our adventures and our prayers

With a thousand recipes, the cutters, the glitter
The colorful frosting on gingerbread people
Always the children's glee

We celebrate the holidays
    We celebrate our friendship
Our cookie marathon of love

Magnanimous Eight

Of what is friendship made
What fabric forms the warmth
The trust of these eight women

So different, yet so alike
Connections woven of simple learning
Learning with abandon the needs of others

In joy and in pain each one takes a step
Venturing into self with one another
Risking the journey

How is friendship nourished, these eight
Challenging each other, understanding self
Note their touch, their praise, their cheers

Expressing life in unique ways
Speaking of hidden pain
The pain of loss, of grief, of fear
Listening and weeping, blessing all
The months, the years move on
The bonds remain

This group has changed
Through death and distance
Memories of their closeness remain

Now only five who pray and love
Who understand the core of life

The Magnanimous Eight

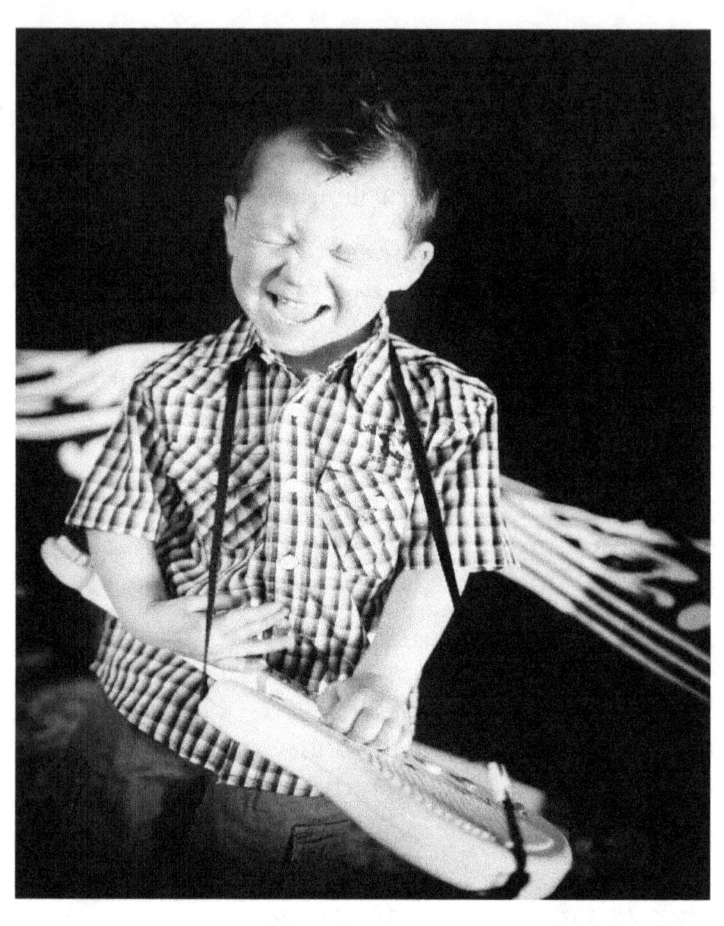

*The ability to express joy is a gift
to ourselves and others*

10

CELEBRATING LIFE

THE celebration of life may take many forms. It is, however, a critical need to each of us. It is an expression of gratitude, an expression of joy, a way to balance the many sad and negative noises that impact our lives. It is a connection vehicle to others, even a way of learning.

Celebrate: rejoice, thankful, free expression
Gratitude: acknowledgement of blessings
Design: blueprint, create a pattern
Simplicity: uncomplicated, without adornment

The sky diver and the opera patron may seem to have little in common as they seek to celebrate life. Each of them, however, is demonstrating freedom of self and spontaneity in celebrating life. The celebration of life is an expression of joy. We bring this joy to birthdays, weddings, accomplishments, and milestones of all kinds - both big and small.

We need no special reasons to celebrate life or the persons in our lives. We can become aware of moments to celebrate every day. A phone call, a hug, a touch, a smile, a note - all can become a celebration of life for ourselves and others. While our culture of extremes often dictates extravagant ways to celebrate life's blessing, simplicity, creativity, and sharing can make any day one of joy.

What do we need to believe in the celebration of life? A positive attitude, a feeling of health, a beautiful day, a cup of coffee or hot chocolate can be a setting. A friendly surprise, a helpful doctor, a thoughtful neighbor or a courteous driver make us pause to rejoice life. We possess many skills to make celebration of our lives a reality. Our unique gifts, our creative spirits, and our trust open our vulnerable side to learn to risk, to reach out, and to lead.

At every age, we can choose to celebrate life:

Youth: with so much to give, whose minds are so creative

Mid-life: whose growing wisdom and life experience demonstrate balance and confidence

Aging: showing us every day that life has meaning in spite of life's inevitable losses. Let's look at some ways to add celebration to our lives:

- Begin with a grateful mindset
- Open ourselves to others: teach them, support them
- Avoid unhappy messages and unhappy people
- Identify simple, creative ways to celebrate: a picnic, a gift, a smile
- Avoid extremes: power, money, perfection, etc.
- Travel near or far: a ride in the Rockies, a trip by train, boat or car
- Create new ways of doing: explore a new path, take a new road
- Seek life's beauty: nature, laughter, a sunset

Life is a gift! Each of us can choose to celebrate our days.

Aging

We can now listen more
    and understand more
We can trust more and accept more
We can touch more and forgive more

We have more faith and more freedom
We have more balance
    and more wisdom
We have more time to laugh
    and to play

Giving up the rush
Giving up the extremes
Giving up foolish pride and power

To notice the beautiful moments
To treasure the beautiful people
To be grateful for a beautiful day

This is our time
To make an impact on our world
To teach and to learn
To embrace life and to model love

Grateful Memories

We hardly notice the years go by
We hardly notice until we speak of memories
With those who have travelled
    the road with us
Our lives are filled with "day to day"
Time controls us but memories remain
    Of laughter
    Of learning and of loving
    Of fervent prayer

Connected by faith, by fate
Connected by our gifts
We remember the smile, the touch
We remember the understanding
We remember the accepting, the forgiving

Though our interaction often lessens
Though life throws us different curve balls
We stay connected in sadness and in joy

We live simple lives with loving hearts
Our friendships are forever
Our memories fill us with gratitude

Magic

It is the jump in my heart when we hug
The spark in my eyes when you call
It is the warmth in my bones when we touch

Celebration happens any day, any moment
Because of tiny things, unrehearsed
Because of being thanked or being noticed

Celebration begins with another
Celebration happens with two or more
Who believe that life can be a celebration

It is magic, it is deliberate
It is birthdays, any day
It is undefined and undeniable

Old memories can be a reason
Making new memories, better still
For celebration, like love, is now

As tree branches live on, so do our voices

JOURNEY SHAPING VOICES

THESE chapters speak of messages - *voices* - that shape our lives. I wish to share some of the many voices that have shaped my own life. They have taught me, loved me, challenged me, and inspired me.

"Love others as you would have them love you" *Jesus*

"You teach the class and I'll observe" *Sylvia, my teacher*

"You heard me, you gave me hope – we did it!" *A client*

"They are wrong, but keep it under your hat" *A mentor*

"Keep your own egg money" *My mother, Ada*

"I respect your choice, we'll get through this together"
	Doctors Vern and George

"Judge your day by the odds against you" *David, a mentor*

"I will cover for you while you do that important task"
	George, a mentor

"Always keep your zest for life, no matter what!" *A dear friend*

"Give your sadness and fears to Him" *A spiritual guide*

Journey Shaping Voices, cont.

"You did it for both of us" *My father, Ronald*

"We remember the first thing you taught us - what it feels like to be loved" *My children*

"Mercy triumphs over judgment" *St. James 2:13*

"Go for it honey, I'll back you all the way" *My husband*

I CHALLENGE EACH OF YOU TO BE SOMEONE'S VOICE!

A POST SCRIPT

IT is a lifelong challenge to learn to interact and to successfully connect with those whose lives we touch. Hopefully, some of the thoughts in *Journey of the Hats* have connected with you, my reader.

Life can bring many dark times which take away our hope. Though no one can completely understand our time of fear and pain, we can reach out to those who, without judgment, care for us. There are wise and gentle people who can serve as teachers, guides, and cheerleaders during our darkest of times.

The world today seems to be more
complicated and harder to navigate than in
the past. It seems to lack trust.
It seems to lack hope. It is not unreasonable,
however, to believe that our children and
their children will create a world that knows
hope and peace.

The universal human spirit seeks the gifts of
love. We find those gifts with each other.

Through both the creative and collaborative
work of bringing *Journey of the Hats* to
life, my cheerleader has been my editor,
Barbara. My gratitude and thanks to her!

Pat

The Mystery of the Clouds

We ride the clouds to our home
To our everyday world
They hail us, tease us, these mounds
   of white fluff

Some are whipped cream islands
And some pavements of snow
Some floating cities
Some ancient castles

Popcorn in heaven-sized bowls
Beautiful angel hair
Icing on a giant's cake
Breathless wedding gown

Others are thick curtains
Hiding miles of souls
Holding energy and dreams
Souls masking hope and hopelessness

Appearing now, the mountains
The clouds caress them
Awesome beauty, setting sun
We whisper our goodbyes

Below are young and old
Day almost done
Unaware of this mystery
The mystery of the clouds